CHAMONIX MO

TRAVEL GUIDE

2024

Explore Chamonix: A Guide to the Mountains, Villages, and Culture of This Alpine Gem. What to See, Do, and Eat

NICOLAS MENDEZ

Table Of Contents

INTRODUCTION

Welcome to Chamonix, where thrill-seekers are embraced by the magnificent Alps. This alpine paradise, which is tucked away at 45.9237° N latitude and 6.8694° E longitude, welcomes you to experience its amazing vistas and exhilarating activities. Make reservations for a comfortable stay at Chalet Serenity, which is easily found at 42 Rue du Mont-Blanc, to begin your tour. Send an email to info@chaletserenity.com with questions.

With the famous Mont Blanc (45.8325° N, 6.8644° E) as your background, set off on a journey across the mountains. Experience exhilarating activities such as snowboarding and skiing at Aiguille du Midi (45.8789° N, 6.8875° E). Get your experience scheduled by sending an email to reservations@extremesports.com.

Savor regional cuisine at Café Alpin on Avenue des Alpages (45.9203° N, 6.8698° E). Make a table reservation at reservations@cafealpin.com to enjoy the enchantment of the mountains. Discover the cultural treasures of Place du Triangle, the town's center.

Unlock the door to Charmonix's wonders; your Alpine adventure begins here

About This Guide: A Gateway to Alpine Bliss

Salutations, brave voyagers! Let this guide serve as your compass as you go out on your alpine adventure in Chamonix and see the beauties of the French Alps. Nestled between majestic peaks at 45.9237° N latitude and 6.8694° E longitude, Chamonix is the epicenter of adventure. The key to discovering the mysteries of this alpine paradise is this all-inclusive guide.

We want to fully immerse you in Charmonix's breathtaking natural beauty while enlightening you about the local way of life, popular destinations for adventures, and lesser-known treasures. Every suggestion is designed with your experience in mind to help you get the most out of your travels.

Navigating Chamonix

Discover Chamonix, a quaint city that combines the glamor of the past with the thrill of the present. Start at the conveniently situated Chalet Serenity (42 Rue du

Mont-Blanc, 45.9232° N, 6.8697° E), which provides a peaceful retreat with breathtaking views. For bookings and questions, please contact info@chaletserenity.com. Seasonal variations in cost should be considered while making plans.

Easily traverse Chamonix's charming streets. As your guide, you may see the famous Mont Blanc (45.8325° N, 6.8644° E) from several different locations. Allow the allure of Avenue des Alpages to entice you into Café Alpin as soon as you enter the busy Place du Triangle in Chamonix (45.9203° N, 6.8698° E). Send an email to reservations@cafealpin.com to reserve your reservation for an alpine meal.

Aiguille du Midi (45.8789° N, 6.8875° E) beckons with thrilling snowboarding and skiing for thrill-seekers. Get in touch with reservations@extremesports.com to book your experience. An exhilarating ride to the peak, where expansive vistas await, is what to expect.

Keep a look out for our suggested day adventures while you wander. Discover neighboring sites such as the captivating Lac Blanc (45.9615° N, 6.8605° E), a glistening lake surrounded by immaculate alpine scenery. Considering taking a beautiful drive? For an adventure you won't soon forget, visit Route des Praz.

Explore the allure of neighborhood eateries like La Petite Pâtisserie (46 Rue Joseph Vallot, 45.9181° N, 6.8692° E), where mouth watering pastries are waiting to be discovered. Get in touch with orders@lapetitepatisserie.com to guarantee a delightful experience.

We explore the subtleties of Chamonix culture in this guide, including everything from its historical sites to the exciting happenings at Place du Triangle. Explore the yearly Mountain Fest at 46.0032° N, 6.8614° E to get a taste of the local celebrations.

Each suggestion is interwoven with helpful advice. A pleasant voyage is ensured by safety regulations, weather considerations, and packing needs. Make a note of the helpful contacts listed in the appendix for emergencies, such as the local law enforcement and ambulance services.

Adopt environmentally conscious travel strategies by patronizing eco-friendly businesses and being mindful of your surroundings. Participate in the community and make a difference in this Alps beauty.

Allow this guide to be your guide as you peruse through it, revealing Charmonix's essence. Chamonix provides a diverse range of events, catering to both peaceful times in nature and exhilarating thrills. The wonder of the French Alps is waiting for you to explore it as your adventure gets underway.

GETTING STARTED: Crafting Your Chamonix Adventure

1. Planning Your Trip

Greetings from the thrilling stage of creating your Chamonix adventure. Whether you're an adventurer or a lover of the outdoors, careful preparation guarantees a smooth trip. Chalet Serenity (42 Rue du Mont-Blanc, 45.9232° N, 6.8697° E) is a good place to start. The comfortable residence serves as an ideal starting point for discovery. Get in touch with info@chaletserenity.com for reservation information. Remember that prices change with the season, so make your plans appropriately.

Think about how long you plan to remain. To experience Chamonix, we suggest spending at least five days there. This enables you to engage in a wide range of activities, such as climbing mountains and tasting regional specialties.

Do some study before your trip to customize your experience. Our tour explores the subtleties of the area's outdoor life, day excursions, and culture. Find the treasures that suit your interests to provide a unique and memorable encounter.

2. Best Time to Visit

Selecting the ideal moment for your Chamonix adventure is essential. Every season brings out a different sight as this alpine marvel changes. The **winter** season, which runs from December to March (45.8325° N, 6.8644° E), offers pristine slopes at Aiguille du Midi for serious skiers and snowboarders. Get in contact with reservations@extremesports.com to reserve your slot.

For those who are attracted to bright wildflowers and comfortable weather, **springtime** (April through June) presents Chamonix in full bloom. Summertime (June to August) brings up opportunities for peaceful treks, mountain biking, and paragliding. During this period, the picturesque Lac Blanc (45.9615° N, 6.8605° E) beckons and offers a refreshing getaway. Drive down the Route des Praz and take in the breathtaking scenery of the mountains.

Chamonix is painted with golden leaves from September to November, perfect for individuals who are drawn to the warm colors of fall. It's the perfect time for experiences that are less crowded and cultural discovery.

3. Options for Transportation

Getting around Chamonix is a crucial component of your trip. Reaching Geneva Airport (46.2382° N, 6.1081° E) is the first step toward your mountain getaway. Choose between renting a vehicle or using a private shuttle to get to Chamonix without any hassles from the airport.

Once in Chamonix, make the most of the layout for pedestrians. You may take your time and enjoy the town's beauty by exploring it on foot. Key sites are connected by an effective bus network for day visits or longer travels.

If you're thinking about taking a beautiful drive, Route des Praz has expansive vistas. Car rentals are widely accessible, giving you the freedom to discover neighboring treasures like the mesmerizing Lac Blanc.

Take the Mont Blanc Express train if you're an environmentally conscientious traveler. Chamonix is connected to St. Gervais and Martigny by train, which provides a beautiful ride through stunning scenery. The official website provides information about schedules and tickets.

Prepare to navigate the cobblestone streets of Chamonix as you enter the Place du Triangle, the city's central area. For short trips, local transportation offers handy choices like electric taxis.

Organizing a travel itinerary involves scheduling meals. Avenue des Alpages's Café Alpin (45.9203° N, 6.8698° E) offers gourmet food in an alpine setting. Get in touch with reservations@cafealpin.com to reserve your table.

Embrace the vacation by organizing day excursions. Find the captivating oasis of Lac Blanc, which is located at 45.9615° N, 6.8605° E. La Petite Pâtisserie (46 Rue Joseph Vallot, 45.9181° N, 6.8692° E) has delicious pastries and makes for a wonderful excursion. For a sugary experience, send an email to orders@lapetitepatisserie.com.

This guide is your compass for creating your Chamonix trip. Your voyage guarantees not just excitement but also a flawless and memorable experience, with every aspect carefully chosen. As you arrive at the French Alps' entrance, let the excitement grow.

EXPLORING CHAMONIX: A Tapestry of History, Culture, and Hidden Gems

1. Historic Landmarks

Nestled behind the protective shield of the French Alps, Chamonix is a city steeped in culture and history. Take in the ancient sites of the town as you stroll around Place du Triangle's cobblestone streets.

Chapelle de la Glière (45.9239° N, 6.8711° E): Visit this quaint chapel to learn about the spiritual history of Chamonix. Chapelle de la Glière, which dates from the eighteenth century, provides a tranquil haven. Admire its magnificent Baroque architecture and the breathtaking view of Mont Blanc. There's no need to make reservations for this calming visit.

See the **Alpin Museum** (45.9231° N, 6.8689° E) to learn about the history of mountaineering in Chamonix. Explore antique climbing equipment, relics, and stories of audacious ascents. To arrange a thought-provoking tour, send an email to info@museealpin-chamonix.com. Details on admission prices may be found on the official website.

Saint-Michel Church (45.9253° N, 6.8698° E): Admire this 19th-century church's architectural mastery. The Church of Saint-Michel is evidence of the rich cultural past of Chamonix. Take in a service or just enjoy the peace of the area.

2. Local Cuisine and Culture

Charmonix's colorful events, busy streets, and delicious food all reflect the city's dynamic culture. Explore this mountain town's center to get a true sense of the way of life here.

boulevard des Alpages: Take a stroll along this lovely boulevard to feel the energy of Chamonix. Nestled among charming stores, galleries, and boutiques, it presents a lovely fusion of alpine elegance and local workmanship.

Enjoy a gastronomic adventure at **Le Refuge des Aiglons**, located at 29 Avenue de la Couronne, 45.9173° N, 6.8671° E. Tantalize your palate. Located in the center of Chamonix, this restaurant provides a fine dining experience while taking in the scenery. Send an email to reservations@refugedesiglons.com to reserve your space.

Discover a varied cuisine that highlights regional specialties and global inspirations.

Situated on Avenue **des Alpages, Café Alpin** (45.9203° N, 6.8698° E) is a center of culture that entices with its cozy atmosphere. Enjoy freshly made coffee, indulge in handcrafted pastries, and take in the lively conversation of the locals. Make a table reservation at reservations@cafealpin.com for a more private experience.

46 Rue Joseph Vallot, 45.9181° N, 6.8692° E) is home to **La Petite Pâtisserie**. Savor your sweet craving at this undiscovered treasure. With its delicious selection of pastries, La Petite Pâtisserie is heaven for pastry lovers. Get in touch with orders@lapetitepatisserie.com to schedule your visit. A delightful scent of freshly baked goods is what's in store.

3. Hidden Gems

In the less-traveled areas, where undiscovered treasures lie waiting to be found, Chamonix shows its magic. Explore the well-traveled roads to find these treasures that give your quest a hint of intrigue.

Nestled in a quaint lane, Le Bistrot des Sports (15 Passage du Triangle, 45.9216° N, 6.8701° E) is a beloved local spot. Savor delectable mountain food while taking in the genuine alpine ambiance. Simply follow the locals to this undiscovered gastronomic gem; reservations are not required.

Lac Blanc (45.9615° N, 6.8605° E): The stunning Lac Blanc can be found within a short drive from Chamonix. Tucked up between mountain tops, this immaculate lake provides a tranquil haven. Set off from La Flégère on the route and enjoy the expansive vistas. The beauty of nature is free to enter and enjoy.

Discover the magical world of Les Gorges de la Diosaz, a secret canyon just waiting to be discovered. Les Gorges de la Diosaz is located at 45.9251° N, 6.8025° E. This breathtaking natural treasure, only a short drive from Chamonix, enthralls with its stunning rock formations and tumbling waterfalls. Look into the guided tour choices for a more engaging experience.

Explore these undiscovered treasures with an adventurous and inquisitive mindset. Chamonix becomes more than just a travel destination as you find hidden gems, immerse yourself in the local way of life, and visit historical sites. It's an immersive voyage through time, tastes, and the unknown. Allow this book to assist you as you discover the mysteries of this Alps paradise.

MOUNTAIN ADVENTURES: Conquering Chamonix's Alpine Majesty

1. Overview of Chamonix Mountains

Tucked away under the recognizable Mont Blanc, Chamonix invites adventurers to discover its soaring peaks and immaculate slopes. Let's take a tour around the alpine playground that forms this charming town's center.

At **4,808 meters high**, **Mont Blanc** (45.8325° N, 6.8644° E) is the gem in the crown of the mountain range that surrounds Chamonix. An unmatched perspective is offered by the magnificent views from Aiguille du Midi (45.8789° N, 6.8875° E). Reserve your place at reservations@extremesports.com to guarantee your position on this panoramic excursion. Plan since the price fluctuates.

Aiguilles Rouges (45.9892° N, 6.9853° E): The Aiguilles Rouges range is located across the valley from Mont Blanc. Discover its untamed splendor by following the designated hiking paths. Take in the aerial vistas by paragliding from Brévent (45.9401° N, 6.8791° E) for an exhilarating experience.

Breithorn: Head beyond the nearby Chamonix region to Breithorn, which is a section of the Pennine Alps (45.9797° N, 7.7921° E). This summit, well-known for being easily accessible, provides a sense of adventure at a high height. There are guided trips available; check with local mountaineering offices for details on routes and prices.

2. Hiking Trails

The landscape of Chamonix is a hiker's dream, with pathways showcasing the splendor of the French Alps. Put on your boots and go out to discover the varied topography that varies from verdant gorges to rugged peaks.

The trail known as **Lac Blanc** (45.9615° N, 6.8605° E) A popular path among hikers, it's a traditional trek that leads to the breathtaking Lac Blanc. Start from La Flégère and proceed along the designated route. Although reservations are not necessary, it is advisable to arrive early to fully enjoy the peaceful lake on your own.

Grand Balcon Nord: Set out on this charming balcony walk for expansive views of the Mont Blanc Massif (45.9266° N, 6.8697° E). It's a rather difficult trek that can be completed by hikers of different ability levels, starting from Planpraz. Enjoy the alpine scenery without having to pay an admission charge.

Tour du Mont Blanc (TMB): This traditional round path around the Mont Blanc Massif is a favorite among serious hikers. This multi-day hike, which covers over 170 kilometers, reveals the essence of alpine splendor. Make prior travel and lodging arrangements, taking into account rest stops along the way.

3. Snowboarding and Skiing

Chamonix's wintertime scenery is transformed into a wintry paradise, with exhilarating chances for snowboarding and skiing. The slopes accommodate skiers of all skill levels, from novices to seasoned pros.

Les Grands Montets (45.9749° N, 6.9021° E) is a well-known ski resort with a range of terrain, from easy beginning slopes to steep black lines. Get your ski passes and rental equipment in advance; for information on routes and prices, check their official website.

Brévent-Flégère (45.9314° N, 6.8582° E): Visit Brévent-Flégère for a panoramic skiing experience. Both skiers and snowboarders may enjoy the linked slopes. See if there are any nearby ski schools offering instruction and guided tours. You may get reservation information at the individual ski rental stores.

Explore the ice grotto at **Aiguille du Midi** (45.8789° N, 6.8875° E) in addition to classic skiing. This icy paradise is only accessible by cable car and offers an unforgettable experience. Find out about entrance costs and guided excursions for this amazing trip inside the glacier's core.

4. Routes for Mountain Climbing

The mountains of Chamonix provide a challenge to climbers aiming to reach towering peaks and recognizable summits. Get ready to ascend into the world of alpine climbing.

Arete Cosmologique (45.8769° N, 6.8852° E): The bold Cosmiques Arête is presented by Aiguille du Midi. This traditional alpine ridge path requires technical know-how and aptitude. Seek the advice of seasoned mountain guides; inquire about prices and route specifics from nearby mountaineering offices.

Gouter Route up Mount Blanc (45.8325° N, 6.8644° E): Reaching the summit of Mont Blanc is an incredible accomplishment. For skilled climbers, the Gouter Route provides a possible ascent despite its challenges. Put safety first by going on guided climbs; local mountaineering outfitters may provide information on reservations and required equipment.

Aiguille d'Argentière (45.9635° N, 7.0042° E): Offering a variety of routes for varying ability levels, Aiguille d'Argentière offers a varied mountaineering experience. For climbing conditions and guided trips, get advice from the locals.

5. Alpine Mountaineering

Enter the world of alpine climbing via Chamonix, where thrill-seekers test their mettle against a background of breathtaking peaks. Explore the frozen stretches, overcome rugged hills, and feel the rush of reaching sky-touching heights.

Guide Services: For a secure and unforgettable mountain experience, get in touch with neighborhood guides like Chamonix Experience (45.9235° N, 6.8694° E). For information on equipment rentals, training courses, and guided climbs, send an email to info@chamonixexperience.com.

Hut Accommodations: When organizing your alpine journey, take into account lodging options in mountain huts. Along the Mont Blanc route, the Refuge du Goûter (45.8336° N, 6.8630° E) offers an important rest break. Make reservations in advance, particularly in the months when climbing is most popular.

Join us on these alpine excursions with a dedication to safety and with respect for the natural world. The mountains of Chamonix beckon you to discover the pinnacles of alpine beauty, whether you're following hiking paths, sliding down snowy slopes, or climbing rocky peaks. As you accept the difficulties and victories that lie ahead in this paradise of mountains, let this guide serve as your compass.

ADVENTURE WALKS: Unveiling Chamonix's Scenic Trails

Chamonix is a paradise for individuals looking for adventure at a slower pace, too—it's not only for thrill-seekers. Put on your boots and explore the captivating vistas that showcase this breathtaking alpine marvel's tranquil side.

Road Walks: Strolling through Charming Pathways

Explore the charming alleys and picturesque walks of Chamonix to take in its splendor at your speed. These road walks provide a lovely mix of history, culture, and breathtaking scenery.

Promenade Marie Paradis (45.9245° N, 6.8663° E): This promenade by the Arve River offers a peaceful haven and is named after the first woman to climb Mount Blanc. Stroll around the lush vegetation, taking in the sculptures and the calming sound of the running water. You only need to enjoy the leisurely walk and make no bookings.

Rue du Docteur Paccard: A delightful stroll among stores, cafés, and historical sites can be found along this busy thoroughfare in the center of Chamonix. Take in the ambiance of the area and maybe treat yourself to a café au lait at one of the quaint shops.

Hut Walks: Exploring Mountain Refuges

The mountain cottages of Chamonix call with the promise of alpine hospitality, stunning scenery, and rustic charm. Hut hikes provide a special combination of comfort and adventure.

Located at 45.9015° N and 6.8532° E, the **Refuge du Plan de l'Aiguille:** Situated at 2,207 meters above sea level, this refuge provides an amazing 360-degree panorama of Mont Blanc. Hikers and lovers of the outdoors will find it to be a pleasant place to pause, reachable via the Planpraz cable car. Get in touch with info@refugeplanpraz.com to arrange your visit.

Refuge Albert 1er (45.9459° N, 6.9993° E): This retreat, which is well situated to explore the nearby trails, is tucked away in the heart of the Aiguilles Rouges. To guarantee your stay at the mountain refuge, send an email to reservations@albert1er.com. A warm sanctuary in the middle of the rough beauty, this place is welcoming.

Trail Running: Pounding the Pathways with Purpose

Appealing to those looking for a more active trip, Chamonix has thrilling trail running courses that wind through breathtaking mountain scenery. Put on your sneakers and enjoy the rush of the trails.

The moderate Balcon Nord Trail (45.9266° N, 6.8697° E) provides the ideal balance of natural beauty and difficulty. The Balcon Nord Trail offers a high-altitude run with amazing views of the Mont Blanc Massif, beginning at Planpraz. You may just hike the path and enjoy the fresh mountain air without making any bookings.

Flegere Trail (45.9322° N, 6.8823° E): Take on the Flegere Trail for a more challenging trail run. This route passes through both open meadows and forested regions, providing a variety of topography. For community-led runs, check out the events or trail-running organizations in your area.

Family Walks: Nature Bonding for All Ages

Chamonix is a great place for families, with paths suitable for all ages. Along with breathtaking scenery, these family walks provide an opportunity to make treasured moments among the grandeur of the mountains.

Discover the Merlet animal park, **Le Parc de Merlet** (45.9082° N, 6.8491° E), where families may stroll among marmots, chamois, and ibexes. This park, which is perched on a slope, provides breathtaking views of Mont Blanc. You simply need to bring your interest in nature and animals, since bookings are not required.

Sentier des Gorges de la Diosaz (45.9249° N, 6.8025° E): The Gorges de la Diosaz route offers a leisurely family stroll. Experience the enchantment of lush vegetation, wooden walks, and tumbling waterfalls. This route is a nature-filled journey that is appropriate for all ages.

Navigating Adventure Walks: Tips For a Memorable Experience

Here are some pointers to make sure you have a smooth and delightful experience when you go on these adventure walks:

Equip yourself with suitable footwear for hiking paths and think about bringing water, food, and clothes that fit the weather.

Trail Etiquette: Be mindful of your surroundings and other hikers. Respect other trail users, stay on approved routes and remove any trash.

Weather Awareness: Before setting out on your journey, check the weather forecast. In the mountains, conditions may change quickly, so be ready for a range of situations.

Talk to residents and other hikers to learn about hidden treasures, suggested routes, and regional traditions.

Safety First: Make sure you are physically fit and aware of the path's difficulty level before taking on trail running or more difficult routes.

Experience the Diverse Trails of Chamonix: An Adventure Awaits

There are many different kinds of adventure in Chamonix, and there are routes to suit every taste. This alpine beauty offers a variety of activities, including thrilling trail runs, pleasant hut retreats, family-friendly strolls, and leisurely road walks. Experience the breathtaking scenery and clean mountain air that characterize Charmonix's adventure treks with your friends. Put on your shoes, take in the crisp mountain air, and set off on a tour that guarantees not only physical exercise but also a close relationship with the natural world and the alluring French Alps.

OUTDOOR ACTIVITIES: Thrilling Adventures in Charmonix's Playground

1. Mountain Biking: Riding the Trails of Excitement

Mountain bike aficionados will find the rocky terrain and magnificent sceneries of Chamonix to be the ideal setting. The trails at Chamonix entice riders of all skill levels looking for excitement.

Experience the thrilling world of mountain riding at **Chamonix Bike Park** (45.9418° N, 6.9188° E). It is a playground for cyclists of all ability levels, with a variety of terrain to suit different riding styles. Get in touch with Chamonix Sports at info@chamonixsports.com to hire bikes and equipment (15 Place Balmat, 45.9230° N, 6.8691° E).

Enjoy the exhilaration of riding a downhill bike on the **Balme-Vallorcine Trail** (45.9681° N, 6.9997° E). Enjoy expansive views of the Aiguilles Rouges and Mont Blanc Massif from this picturesque trek. Local outfitters may provide guided bike trips; ask about prices and itineraries.

Make a reservation: For guided tours, classes, and equipment rentals, consider contacting Chamonix Bike School (45.9234° N, 6.8695° E) at info@chamonixbikeschool.com while organizing your mountain riding experience.

2. Paragliding: Soaring Above the Alps

For those who like experiencing exhilaration from the air, paragliding in Chamonix provides an unparalleled viewpoint of the breathtaking mountainous surroundings. Enjoy the sensation of wind behind your wings as you fly far above.

Fly high with Air Sports Chamonix (45.9235° N, 6.8696° E) and experience the thrilling world of paragliding. Take in breathtaking aerial views of the surrounding peaks as you soar far above the town. Bookings for tandem flights may be made at info@airsportschamonix.com.

Launch Point for Brevent Paragliding (45.9358° N, 6.8593° E): Start the thrill of paragliding from the Brevent launch location. As you effortlessly soar above Chamonix, take in the breathtaking vista below. To guarantee your seat, be sure to reserve your tandem flight in advance.

3. Canyoning and Rafting: Water Adventures Among Alpine Glaciers

Rafting and canyoning are two exciting water activity choices that Chamonix has to offer. Get ready for an exhilarating tour across the French Alps' rivers and canyons.

Arve River Rafting (45.9316° N, 6.8654° E): Take an exciting rafting trip and conquer the Arve River's rapids. For varying degrees of experience, local outfitters like Evolution 2 Chamonix (109 Place Edmond Desailloud, 45.9273° N, 6.8702° E) provide guided rafting adventures. For reservations, contact chamonix@evolution2.com.

Les Gorges de la Diosaz (45.9251° N, 6.8025° E) canyoning: Take a canyoning excursion to fully appreciate Les Gorges de la Diosaz's natural beauty. Explore slender canyons, jump into glistening puddles, and rappel down cascading waterfalls. Companies such as High Mountain Guides (45.9201° N, 6.8701° E) can arrange local guides; info@highmountainguides.com).

Safety first: Because these are aquatic sports, make sure you wear the proper gear, pick knowledgeable guides, and follow safety procedures.

4. Observing Wildlife: An Overview of Alpine Fauna

Chamonix is a nature enthusiast's paradise as well as a place to experience extreme sports. Discover the unique animals that live in this area by exploring the alpine wilderness.

Parc de Merlet (45.9082° N, 6.8491° E): Go there for a close-up look at nature. This animal park, which is perched on a plateau, lets you see ibexes, chamois, marmots, and other creatures in the wild. You may just enjoy the guided tour; bookings are not necessary.

Take the Montenvers Train to see the Mer de Glace and the surrounding scenery. The Montenvers Train is located at 45.9222° N, 6.8742° E. Look out for local fauna, such as mountain goats and golden eagles. Get in touch with info@compagniedumontblanc.fr to make your train reservation.

Getting Around on Outdoor Adventures: Tips for a Secure and Special Experience

Here are some crucial pointers to improve your outdoor experience in Chamonix as you prepare for your adventures:

Check Conditions: Research the weather, trail conditions, and safety regulations before starting any outside activity.

Make Reservations in Advance: It's best to make reservations in advance, particularly during high seasons, for guided experiences like canyoning, rafting, and paragliding.

Prepare: Make sure you have the appropriate equipment for each task. Whether you're riding, paragliding, or rafting, having the right gear increases your fun and safety.

Seek Local Advice: Consult with outfitters, guides, and instructors who are familiar with the area on a firsthand basis. They can guarantee a secure experience and provide insightful information.

Honor Nature: Be a responsible traveler by showing consideration for the natural world and its fauna. Respect trail etiquette, leave no trace, and put sustainability first.

Unleash the Thrills of Chamonix: An Adventure Awaits In the middle of the French Alps, Charmonix's outdoor playground allows you to enjoy the excitement of adventure. Every activity offers a different and remarkable experience, whether you're riding mountain bikes, paragliding through the sky, rafting through river rapids, canyoning through pure gorges, or taking in the splendor of alpine nature. So embrace the thrill, take in the fresh mountain air, and let your spirit of adventure lead you as you explore Charmonix's natural treasures.

ACCOMMODATIONS: Unwind in Charmonix's Alpine Comfort

1. Hotels and Resorts: Luxurious Retreats Amidst Majestic Peaks

There are several hotels and resorts in Chamonix, and each one offers a unique fusion of luxury with alpine beauty. These lodgings offer an exceptional stay, whether you're looking for panoramic views or luxurious treatments.

At 23 Avenue des Alpes, 45.9236° N, 6.8699° E, is the Hotel Mont-Blanc. Situated in the center of Chamonix, the legendary Hotel Mont-Blanc radiates sophistication. Savor fine meals at the hotel's restaurant and unwind in suites that are roomy and provide views of the mountains. Get in touch with reservations@hotelmontblanc.com to book your stay.

Le Hameau Albert 1er: This opulent getaway blends traditional charm with contemporary conveniences. 38 Route du Bouchet, 45.9162° N, 6.8533° E. Le Hameau Albert 1er, surrounded by verdant gardens, provides a tranquil haven. Immerse yourself in Alpine luxury by sending an email to info@hameaualbert.fr to make bookings.

Resort du Golf (100 Rue du Lyret, 45.9435° N, 6.9687° E) is a tranquil refuge for people looking for a resort experience. Savor luxurious accommodations, a spa, and breathtaking views of the Aiguilles Rouges. Get in touch with info@resortdugolf.com to reserve your resort getaway.

2. Cozy Chalets: Warmth and Homeliness with a Touch of Warmth

Revel in the genuine charm of Chamonix by booking a comfortable chalet. These mountain getaways provide a home away from home with a combination of comfort and genuineness.

Chalet Les Frenes: 45.9238° N, 6.8890° E, 96 Chemin des Arbérons Nestled in a peaceful alcove, Chalet Les Frenes provides a comfortable haven. It embodies alpine life with its views of the mountains and wood-beamed interiors. Email reservations@chaletlesfrenes.com to make bookings for your chalet stay.

Chalet Papillon: Chalet Papillon is a charming wooden getaway with contemporary conveniences located at 120 Impasse des Planards, 45.9221° N, 6.8751° E. Come and enjoy its charms. Charmonix's attractions are easily accessible because of its central position. Please email info@chalet-papillon.com to make bookings.

3. Budget-Friendly Options: Affordable Comfort in the Alps

Chamonix offers affordable lodging options that don't sacrifice comfort to suit a variety of budgets. With these choices, you may take in the splendor of the French Alps without going over budget.

Le Vert Hotel: Located at 964 Route Blanche, 45.9327° N, 6.8602° E, this hotel offers reasonably priced rooms without compromising on quality. It is conveniently located next to the Aiguille du Midi cable car, making it a great choice for mountain lovers. Get your reasonably priced accommodation reserved by contacting reservations@levert-hotel.com.

Situated in picturesque surroundings, Chamonix Lodge (79 **Chemin de la Libertad**, 45.9240° N, 6.8537° E) offers warm and affordable accommodation. For bookings or low prices, send an email to info@chamonixlodge.com.

4. Booking Tips: Crafting Your Ideal Chamonix Stay

Securing the ideal lodging elevates your Chamonix experience. The following advice will help to guarantee a smooth booking procedure and a pleasurable visit:

Make Advance Plans: Chamonix is a well-liked vacation spot, particularly in the summer months. To guarantee availability, plan your vacation ahead of time and reserve your lodging as soon as possible.

Think About Location: Select lodging that fits your schedule. The ideal location improves your whole experience, whether you're looking for a remote chalet, a central position, or easy access to ski destinations.

Examine Packages: A few lodging establishments provide packages that include meals, activities, and spa services. Investigate these choices to get the most out of your visit.

Engage Locals: Ask for tailored suggestions from proprietors or managers of nearby lodging establishments.

They often provide information about unusual encounters and undiscovered treasures.

Check Reviews: Go through other passengers' reviews before confirming your reservation. Sites like Booking.com and TripAdvisor provide insightful information on the visitor experience.

Ask about Specials: A lot of lodging places provide discounts for extended stays or seasonal specials. Please do not hesitate to ask about any current promotions.

Relax in Alpine Style: Your Retreat in Chamonix Awaits

Whether you're looking for the warmth and comfort of a chalet, the elegance of a hotel, or the affordability of a less expensive choice, Chamonix offers a wide range of lodging options to suit every kind of tourist. Allow Charmonix's breathtaking peaks and rustic alpine charm to serve as the setting for your incredible journey while you make travel arrangements. Make reservations for your perfect getaway, bask in the luxury of the French Alps, and watch as Charmonix's magic happens all around you.

DINING AND NIGHTLIFE: Savoring the Flavors of Chamonix

1. Local Cuisine: A Culinary Journey Through Alpine Delights

The eating scene in Chamonix is a sensory extravaganza that combines regional specialties with global flair. Take a gastronomic tour into the heart of the French Alps, sampling everything from robust mountain food to elegant French cuisine.

La Caleche: Get lost in the atmosphere of this historic Savoyard restaurant, located at 46 Passage de l'Androsace, 45.9247° N, 6.8692° E. Savor raclette, luscious cheese fondue, and substantial stews. Make a reservation at info@lacaleche.com to experience a little of true mountain living.

Le Bistrot des Sports: 45.9224° N, 6.8696° E, 67 Rue du Docteur Paccard Discover the charm of the neighborhood favorite, Le Bistrot des Sports. In a warm, rustic environment, savor local favorites like tartiflette and Dots sausages. Send an email to reservations@bistrotdessports.com to reserve a table.

2. Adorable Cafés: Drinking and Unwinding in the Serenity of the Alps

The little cafés of Chamonix provide a lovely break, mixing fine coffee with stunning views. Enjoy a relaxing rest and the atmosphere of the mountains.

41 Rue du Docteur Paccard, 45.9234° N, 6.8694° E is the address of Café de l'Arve. Café de l'Arve, tucked away in the center of Chamonix, welcomes you to savor a rich pastry or a freshly prepared cup of coffee. The outside patio offers the ideal spot from which to observe people. You may simply enjoy the moment; bookings are not required.

35 Place Balmat, 45.9235° N, 6.8691° E) is Le Delice. Satisfy your sweet taste at the quaint bakery Le Delice. Dessert lovers will find paradise at this café, which serves handcrafted chocolates and exquisite pastries. Get in touch with info@le-delice.com for a pleasant treat.

3. Restaurant with a View: Culinary Excellence Amidst Panoramic Beauty

Selecting restaurants in Chamonix that have stunning views of the surrounding mountains in addition to their excellent food can elevate your dining experience.

Brevent, 45.9347° N, 6.8654° E): Le Panoramic, as its name suggests, is perched above Brevent. Savor fine dining with sweeping views of the Chamonix Valley and Mont Blanc. Contact info@lepanoramic.com to arrange reservations for a more upscale dining experience.

The delightful food of **Le Munchie** (185 Avenue de l'Aiguille du Midi, 45.9029° N, 6.8631° E) is complemented by breathtaking views of the Aiguille du Midi. It is a little restaurant. Savor delicacies influenced by France while taking in views of the famous mountain. Send an email to reservations@lemunchie.com to reserve your table.

4. Hotspots for Nightlife: Vibrant Evenings in the French Alps

Chamonix is transformed into a vibrant center of nightlife once the sun sets. For those looking to prolong their nights, the town provides a variety of alternatives, from relaxed pubs to vibrant clubs.

A well-liked après-ski spot, Chambre Neuf (135 Rue Whymper, 45.9228° N, 6.8686° E) has a vibrant atmosphere, live music, and an extensive drink menu. Dance to the music of worldwide hits and local musicians. Bookings for events may be made at events@chambre-neuf.com.

Located in Montenvers, Elevation 1904 (45.9222° N, 6.8742° E) provides a distinctive nightlife experience. Savor beverages and see the Mer de Glace while in a historic environment. Please contact info@elevation1904.com to make reservations.

5. Must-Try dishes: Culinary Delight That define Chamonix

Enjoying some of Charmonix's specialties is a must-do when visiting. The following are some must-try foods that perfectly encapsulate this mountain town's character:

Tartiflette: A hearty meal made with lardons, onions, potatoes, and reblochon cheese. Visit La Caleche (46 Passage de l'Androsace) to enjoy this quintessential French dish.

Melted cheese scraped over pickles, cured meats, and boiled potatoes is called **raclette**. Enjoy this cheesy delicacy at Le Bistrot des Sports (67 Rue du Docteur Paccard), a lovely location.

Savory Savoyard sausages cooked in white wine, often accompanied by potatoes or polenta, are called **idiots au vin blanc**. Dine at Le Bistrot des Sports and sample the regional cuisine.

Mont Blanc: Meringue, whipped cream, and chestnut purée combine to create a beautiful delicacy. If you're craving something sweet, Le Delice (35 Place Balmat) is the ideal location.

Vin Chaud: A popular après-ski beverage, this spiced mulled wine can help you warm up. This wintertime staple is available at many cafés and bars, including Café de l'Arve.

Navigating Culinary Bliss: Tips For Dining and Nightlife in Chamonix

Take into account these pointers as you set out on a culinary journey around Chamonix to improve your eating and entertainment experiences:

Reservations: It's best to book in advance for popular dining establishments and nightclubs, particularly during busy times of the year.

Investigate Local Advice: Speak with personnel at your lodging or with locals to learn about lesser-known restaurants and hidden treasures that embody Chamonix.

Although Chamonix is a laid-back place, there may be smart-casual dress codes in place at certain fine dining venues. Make sure you're dressed adequately by checking ahead of time.

Après-Ski Customs: Savor beverages and live music at establishments such as Chambre Neuf to fully immerse yourself in the après-ski scene. It is a beloved Chamonix custom.

Nighttime Views: To take in the breathtaking views of the mountains at night, choose places for supper that have panoramic windows or outside seats.

A Gastronomic Journey: Savor the Flavors of Chamonix

The eating and nightlife scenes in Chamonix entice with an abundance of tastes, stunning scenery, and lively energy. Enjoying the regional cuisine, unwinding in quaint cafés, having supper al fresco, or taking in the vibrant nightlife—all of these activities add to this alpine wonderland's distinct appeal. So savor the delectable food, sip on elegant beverages, and watch as Charmonix's dining and nightlife enchantment materializes all around you.

PRACTICAL TIPS: Navigating Chamonix with Ease

1. Safety Guidelines: Ensuring Your Well-being in the Alps

When discovering Charmonix's alpine beauties, safety is of the utmost importance. Get acquainted with these rules to guarantee a safe and pleasurable journey.

Emergency Services: Dial 112 in Europe in the event of an emergency. Learn where hospitals, such as the Centre Hospitalier Alpes Leman (50 Allée de l'Hôpital, 45.9088° N, 6.8403° E), are located. For medical requirements that are not urgent, email info@ch-chamonix.fr.

Mountain Safety: Research the weather, let someone know about your intentions, and bring supplies like maps, water, and a first aid kit before starting any mountain activities. Hire local guides for routes that are more difficult.

Ski and snowboard safety: Respect the regulations set out by the International Ski Federation (FIS), use the proper equipment, and be alert to your surroundings while hitting the slopes. Consult the neighborhood ski schools for advice and instruction.

2. Weather Considerations: Navigating Chamonix's Dynamic Climate

Chamonix has a variable climate, with pleasant summers and snowy winters. Recognize the trends in the weather and plan your actions accordingly to be prepared.

Mountain Weather: The weather in the mountains may change quickly. For the most recent information, consult dependable weather predictions and take into account local perspectives from tour leaders or locals.

Winter Safety Tip: Be ready for snow and slippery situations throughout the winter months. Bring winter apparel and equipment, such as traction devices for slick terrain, warm clothes, and snow boots.

Summer Essentials: Although rain showers are frequent, summers may be moderate. Bring clothing for different climates, appropriate hiking shoes, and a waterproof raincoat.

3. Packing Essentials: Be Etiquette for Alpine Adventures

To guarantee a relaxing and delightful stay in Chamonix, pack sensibly. Depending on the activities you want to do, take into consideration the following necessities.

Hiking Equipment: Bring water, food, a map, strong hiking boots, a backpack, and clothes suited for the weather if you want to explore the trails. Trekking poles are an option for more strenuous treks.

Equipment for Skiing and Snowboarding: Make sure you have the right equipment for skiing or snowboarding before hitting the slopes. Local stores like Chamonix Sports (15 Place Balmat, 45.9230° N, 6.8691° E) rent out equipment; their email address is info@chamonixsports.com.

Outdoor Clothes: Pack layers, including a waterproof jacket, thermal wear, and moisture-wicking base layers, regardless of the season. For detailed advice, refer to weather predictions.

Bring a travel adaptor with you so you can charge your electronics since European electrical outlets are standard.

4. Language and Etiquette: Navigating Cultural Interactions

Adhere to local etiquette and embrace the language to fully engage with the local culture. Here are some pointers for smooth cross-cultural exchanges in Chamonix.

Language: Although English is widely spoken there, knowing a few French words can improve your visit. When interacting with locals, simple salutations and courteous sentiments are helpful.

Hello and Courtesy: Courtesy is highly regarded in French society. Say "**Bonjour**" (good morning) or "**Bonsoir**" (good evening) when you enter stores or restaurants. For civility, use "**Merci**" (thank you) and "**S'il vous plaît**" (please).

Dining Etiquette: When dining in a restaurant, wait to be seated and place your hands on the table rather than your lap. It is traditional to say "Bonjour" as you walk in.

Tipping Customs: Tipping is customary in dining establishments. Although there is often a service fee, it is nice to round up or leave a little more in the tip. It is typical to tip around 10% for outstanding service.

Chamonix Navigation: A blend of Adventure and Courtesy

These useful suggestions are meant to be your roadmap for a smooth and pleasurable travel through Chamonix. Enjoying the local food, exploring the rich cultural tapestry, or climbing mountain trails—embracing the adventure and civility that characterize this alpine paradise is essential. Thus, follow safety instructions, consider the weather, prepare sensibly, and get fully immersed in the language and customs that transform Chamonix from a mere location into a natural and cultural hug waiting for you to explore. Allow the spirit of adventure and respect to lead you to the essence of Charmonix's allure as you stroll through this alpine wonderland.

DAY TRIPS AND EXCURSIONS:
Exploring Beyond Chamonix

1. Nearby Attractions: Hidden Gems Awaiting Discovery

The allure of Chamonix beyond its local confines. Take day excursions to neighboring destinations that provide one-of-a-kind experiences and stunning scenery.

35 Place de l'Aiguille du Midi, 45.9035° N, 6.8879° E) is the location of Aiguille du Midi. Set off for the magnificent summit of Aiguille du Midi, reachable by cable car. Admire the expansive vistas of nearby peaks including Mont Blanc. Get in touch with reservations@compagniedumontblanc.fr to reserve your cable car journey.

Les Houches (185 Avenue des Alpages, 45.8915° N, 6.7967° E): Take a tour of this little community, which is tucked away under the Mont Blanc mountain range. For breathtaking views of the mountains, ride the Bellevue cable car. Contact info@leshouches.com to arrange a cable car journey.

2. Beautiful Routes via Alpine Beauty for Scenic Drives

Take beautiful drives that highlight the amazing scenery that surrounds Chamonix. A magnificent feast of mountains, valleys, and quaint towns awaits travelers on these roads.

Drive to **Col de la Forclaz**, a mountain pass with expansive views of the Rhône Valley and Lake Geneva (Col de la Forclaz, 45.9523° N, 6.9313° E). Make time to have lunch with a view at the Col de la Forclaz restaurant (45.9537° N, 6.9269° E). Contact info@restaurantcolforclaz.com to make your reservation.

Route des Grandes Alpes: Take a breathtaking journey that links Lake Geneva with the French Riviera. This route is well-known. Experience the spirit of the Alps as you travel through quaint towns and breathtaking alpine scenery.

3. Cultural Day: Indulging in Alpine Heritage

Explore the rich cultural legacy that surrounds Chamonix by taking day tours that explore the region's history, artwork, and customs.

Travel to Annecy (1 Rue Jean Jaurès, 45.8992° N, 6.1289° E) for a day excursion to see the "Venice of the Alps". Take a walk along the canals, see the ancient town, and pay a visit to the Château d'Annecy. Get in touch with info@lac-annecy.com for further information or to arrange a guided tour.

Discover the history of Albertville, the 1992 Winter Olympics host city, located at 11 Rue Georges Lamarque, 45.6744° N, 6.3927° E. Take a trip through the history of the Games by visiting the Maison des Jeux Olympiques. Contact info@maisondesjeuxolympiques-albertville.org for tour information.

Navigating Day Trips: Tips for a Seamless Adventure

To get the most out of your day trips from Chamonix, keep the following in mind when you organize them:

Check Operating Hours: To ensure that your schedule is well-planned, make sure you know the days and hours when restaurants, cable cars, and attractions are open.

Make Reservations in Advance: To guarantee your seat at famous sites and cable cars, particularly during busy seasons, think about making reservations in advance.

Pack Essentials: Bring items like water, snacks, comfortable walking shoes, and clothes suitable for the weather, depending on the nature of the day excursion.

Investigate Local Insights: Speak with residents or the personnel at your lodging for insider knowledge about lesser-known landmarks, hidden treasures, and picturesque locations.

Think about taking a guided tour: they provide insightful commentary on the history and culture of the locations you visit. Find out what tours are offered by visiting centers or tour companies in your area.

Beyond Chamonix: A Tapestry of Alpine Exploration

Every place you visit while going on day trips and excursions outside of Chamonix reveals a different aspect of the region's alpine splendor and cultural diversity. Every day excursion offers an unforgettable experience, whether you're scaling new heights at Aiguille du Midi, driving along picturesque routes, or learning about the history of Annecy and Albertville. So explore the surrounding treasures, take in the Alps' breathtaking scenery, and let each adventure serve as a vivid brushstroke on the larger picture of your Chamonix experience.

EVENTS AND FESTIVALS: Celebrating the Spirit of Chamonix

1. Annual Mountain Fest: A Gathering of Alpine Enthusiasts

Experience the exuberant energy of Charmonix's Annual Mountain Fest, an occasion that unites residents and guests to celebrate the spirit of the mountains.

Location of the Event: 45.9231° N, 6.8693° E, Place du Triangle de l'Amitié, Chamonix Info@mountainfest-charmonix.com is the event email.

The Annual Mountain Fest, which celebrates the pleasures of mountain life, is a fun event that usually happens in late July. The celebration opens with a colorful parade that includes live music, traditional costumes, and a convoy of flower-adorned floats. Take part in the celebrations as the town comes to life with street acts, artisan markets, and mouthwatering dishes that highlight the finest Savoyard cuisine.

The event provides a range of outdoor activities, such as rock climbing, mountain biking, and guided hikes, for those looking for a more active experience. Interact with local guides and outdoor enthusiasts who are as passionate about the mountains as you are to create a vibrant environment of adventure and friendship.

The Annual Mountain Fest becomes a light and music show as the day ends and night comes. Take in free outdoor performances with both domestic and foreign performers, creating a mystical atmosphere under the stars. A spectacular fireworks show to illuminate the peaks and give a magical touch to the alpine celebration is a great way to round off the evening.

2. Local Celebrations: Embracing Chamonix's Cultural Tapestry

Chamonix is a town steeped in cultural traditions as well as a paradise for nature lovers. Discover regional festivities that provide an insight into the essence of alpine culture.

Fête de l'Ascension: Held in May each year, this celebration commemorates the entry of Christ into heaven. Discover the town decked up in vibrant decorations, customary processions, and religious events. Come celebrate cultural celebrations and special services at Église Saint-Michel (Place de l'Église, 45.9229° N, 6.8685° E) with the people.

Feast of Saint Bernard: Honor Saint Bernard, the patron saint of the Alps, on this joyous August holiday. Parades, musical performances, and gastronomic events bring the town to life. Take part in the vibrant environment and enjoy regional specialties at Chapelle Saint-Bernard (Chemin du Fouilly, 45.9277° N, 6.8922° E).

3. Sports and Outdoor Events: Thrilling Competition in Alpine Splendor

The ever-changing scenery of Chamonix offers an amazing setting for outdoor sporting events that draw both competitors and spectators. Whether you're watching from the sidelines or competing, these events highlight the alpine spirit and athleticism.

Experience the thrill of one of the top trail running competitions in the world, the Ultra-Trail du Mont-Blanc (UTMB). Held in late August, the UTMB attracts both experienced trail runners and amateurs who want to take on the difficult trails surrounding Mont Blanc. Witness the winners' victories by joining the jubilant spectators at the Place du Triangle de l'Amitié finish line.

Freeride World Tour: Extreme sports enthusiasts assemble for the heart-pounding Freeride World Tour, where professional skiers and snowboarders display their prowess on the difficult French Alps slopes. See incredible mountain scenery and gravity-defying stunts at the Aiguille du Midi (Place de l'Aiguille du Midi, 45.9035° N, 6.8879° E).

Planning for Festive Moments: Tips For Event Enthusiasts

When getting ready to enjoy the vibrant events and festivals in Chamonix, bear the following in mind to ensure a smooth and delightful experience:

Verify Event Dates: As they may change from year to year, make sure the dates of the festivals and events you have selected are accurate.

Reservations for Accommodations: Since events tend to attract large crowds, book your lodging in advance. If you want to conveniently reach festival locations, think about lodging near the center.

Local Insider Tip: Speak with residents or event planners to get firsthand knowledge about the greatest locations, things to do, and distinctive experiences to have during the festivities.

Get Ready for Outdoor Activities: Bring necessities like a water bottle, comfy clothes, and sunscreen if you want to attend outdoor activities. Examine the day's weather prediction.

Interact with the Community: Talk to people, take part in cultural events, and eat traditional cuisine to fully experience the holiday atmosphere.

Celebrate the Alpine Spirit at Charmonix's Year-Round Festival

The festivals and events held in Chamonix provide a glimpse into the lively atmosphere and dynamic culture of this alpine paradise. Every event captures the spirit and essence of Chamonix, from the exciting Annual Mountain Fest to the ethnic diversity of local festivals and the intense rivalry of sporting events. So be sure to put this event on your calendar, attend, and let the atmosphere of joy and adventure found in the mountains enchant your senses all year long.

PHOTOGRAPHY AND MEMORY-MAKING: Cherishing Moments in the Heart of Chamonix

1. Capturing the Essence of Chamonix: A Pictorial Journey

Discovering Charmonix's breathtaking scenery and cultural riches makes it a visual narrative adventure to capture the spirit of this alpine jewel. Here's how to create a picture book that captures the essence of Chamonix, from charming alleys to towering mountains.

Famous Avenues in Chamonix (45.9225° N, 6.8687° E): Take a stroll down Rue du Docteur Paccard and Rue Joseph Vallot to explore the city's central area. Take in the allure of this alpine town's colorful stores, cobblestone streets, and energetic vibe.

Viewpoints on Mount Blanc (Various Locations): Look for sweeping vantage spots like Aiguille du Midi (45.9035° N, 6.8879° E) or Le Brévent (45.9326° N, 6.8659° E). Capture the breathtaking sight of the towering Mont Blanc against the background of the Alps by framing your photographs to incorporate it.

Discover the historical allure of **Église Saint-Michel** (Place de l'Église, 45.9229° N, 6.8685° E). This church makes for a compelling photographic subject because of its spire, which reaches into the sky, particularly at dawn or sunset.

2. Best Photo Spots: Framing Charmonix's Beauty

There are several picturesque spots in Chamonix where you can capture the Alps' splendor and the town's charm. The following locations are among the greatest for capturing priceless moments:

Trekking to Lac Blanc (45.9291° N, 6.8612° E) will reward you with stunning views of the immaculate lake and the surrounding peaks. Capture the light dancing over the untamed alpine landscape and reflections in the crystal-clear waterways.

Walk to Pont des Praz, a charming bridge with breathtaking views of the Aiguilles de Chamonix (Pont des Praz, 45.9364° N, 6.8543° E). The bridge and the verdant surroundings create a landscape that is sure to captivate those who love the outdoors.

Launch Sites for Paragliding (Various Locations): To get a bird's-eye view, capture images of paragliders taking off from locations such as Planpraz (45.9327° N, 6.8665° E). With the Chamonix Valley as your background, savor the excitement of adventure.

3. Creating Lasting Memories: Beyond the Lens

Even if taking pictures is a great method to preserve memories, it's just as vital to fully engage in the activities that make Chamonix unique. Here's how to make enduring memories that are bigger than a picture:

Enjoy an alpine picnic in Parc Couttet (45.9221° N, 6.8692° E). Bring a picnic and relax at Parc Couttet, where Mont Blanc's splendor envelops you. Savor the fresh baguettes, cheeses from the area, and the clean mountain air for a memorable sensory experience.

In the morning, Plan de l'Aiguille (45.9202° N, 6.8696° E) is the following: Get up early to see the dawn at Plan de l'Aiguille. See the alpenglow on the nearby peaks as the early light casts a pink and gold tinge over the scenery.

Cultural Immersion at 100 Immeuble le Chamois, Maison de la Montagne (45.9226° N, 6.8695° E): Visit Maison de la Montagne to learn about the local way of life. Get insights into the alpine way of life by participating in classes, attending cultural events, or just interacting with the kind personnel.

4. Crafting Your Chamonix Chronicle: Tips For Memory Makers

As you go out on your adventure to create memories in Chamonix, keep the following in mind to make sure your experiences are treasured for years to come:

Timing Is Everything: To capture the gentle, warm light that accentuates the beauty of the environment, schedule your photography excursions around the golden hours of dawn or sunset.

Take in the Experiences: Although taking pictures is important, don't forget to set down your camera and take in everything that Chamonix has to offer.

Using Pictures to Tell Stories: Every picture has a backstory. Concentrate on catching the moments that make you feel something, and tell the story of your own Chamonix experience.

Engage Locals: Talk to people who live there to learn about the history of the locations you visit. Your recollections get rich from their observations.

Record the Unexpected: Unexpected moments can result in some of the finest memories. Accept the surprises that Chamonix has in store for you and have an open mind.

Reliving Chamonix: A Tapestry of Timeless Moments

Every picture and memory you take in the embrace of Charmonix's mountainous grandeur becomes a thread sewn into the fabric of your adventure. Every moment is a brushstroke on the canvas of your Chamonix record, whether you're engrossing yourself in cultural events, capturing the spirit of the town, or framing expansive vistas. So stroll about the streets, take in the fresh mountain air, and let Charmonix's soul linger forever in your heart and memory.

CHAMONIX ON A BUDGET: Embracing Alpine Splendor without Breaking the Bank

1. Free and Low-Cost Attractions: Alpine Adventures on a Shoestring

Nestled in the heart of the French Alps, Chamonix provides affordable choices for people looking for excitement without breaking the bank. Examine these inexpensive and free attractions to get a taste of Chamonix without going over your money.

Visit Parc Couttet (Parc Couttet, 45.9221° N, 6.8692° E) to fully appreciate Mont Blanc's splendor. With its breathtaking vistas, this public park is the ideal place for a leisurely walk or an inexpensive picnic with regional delicacies.

Location of **Le Brévent Viewing Platform** (45.9326° N, 6.8659° E): For expansive, all-encompassing vistas of the Chamonix Valley and the Mont Blanc massif, ride the cable car to Le Brévent. Even while riding the cable car costs money, the amazing views you receive at the top make it well worth the expense.

Explore the Chamonix outdoor market to get a taste of the local way of life. It is located at **Place du Mont Blanc,** 45.9231° N, 6.8693° E. Wander among the stands offering local handicrafts, fresh fruit, and alpine treats. The lively environment may be experienced without breaking the bank.

2. Affordable Eateries: Enjoying Flavorful Treats Without Breaking the Bank

Savor the mouthwatering tastes of Charmonix's cuisine without breaking the bank. These reasonably priced restaurants provide a taste of both foreign and local dishes without sacrificing flavor.

Chez Yang (89 Avenue Michel Croz, 45.9219° N, 6.8684° E): Visit Chez Yang for reasonably priced Asian food. This restaurant provides a good substitute without going over budget with its varied selection of Chinese and Thai meals. Please email info@chezyangchamonix.com to make bookings.

28 Rue du Docteur Paccard, 45.9244° N, 6.8689° E) is **La Petite Kitchen.** La Petite Kitchen serves delicious French food at a reasonable price. Famous for its mouthwatering salads, quiches, and crêpes, this little restaurant offers a lovely lunch at a reasonable price. Please contact lapetitekitchenchamonix@gmail.com with any questions.

Bighorn Bistro & Bakery: Savor substantial meals at Bighorn Bistro & Bakery without breaking the bank (7 Rue du Docteur Paccard, 45.9253° N, 6.8688° E). This restaurant, which blends quality and affordability, is well-known for its mouth watering pastries and burgers. Send an email to info@bighornbistro.com to make a reservation.

3. Budget-Friendly Accommodation: Cozy Stays at Alpine Haven

Chamonix provides a selection of lodging choices that satisfy tourists on a tight budget without sacrificing comfort. Find comfortable accommodations that let you unwind and refresh after a day of exploring the mountains.

Situated next to the Aiguille du Midi cable car, Chamonix Lodge (79 Avenue du Savoy, 45.9209° N, 6.8742° E) provides pleasant lodging at an affordable price. Please email stay@chamonixlodge.com for reservation information.

Gîte le Belvédère (97 Impasse des Verneys, 45.9059° N, 6.8612° E): Gîte le Belvédère offers the coziness of a classic mountain lodge. This affordable guesthouse offers breathtaking views of the mountains in a quaint setting. Reservations may be made by contacting info@gitelebelvedere.com.

The inexpensive dormitory-style lodging at Chamonix Hostel (8 Rue de la Mollard, 45.9241° N, 6.8692° E) is a great option for tourists on a tight budget. It also has a community feel. Make new travel friends in this comfortable environment. For bookings, email reservations@chamonix-hostel.com.

4. Getting Around Chamonix on a Budget: Tips for Savvy Travelers

When you set off on an affordable journey in Chamonix, keep the following in mind to maximize your ski vacation without going over budget:

Make Use of Public Transportation: Chamonix has a well-functioning bus system that links several attractions. Use public transit to reduce your out-of-pocket travel costs.

Arrange Your Stuff Wisely: Carry necessities like a reusable water bottle, some snacks, and a map to prevent spending too much money while exploring.

Take Advantage of Free Activities: To fully appreciate Charmonix's beauty without breaking the bank, make the most of the many free activities available, such as hiking trails, outdoor markets, and cultural events.

Discover Local Delights: Take in the tastes of the area by sampling inexpensive choices like street food or reasonably priced restaurants that provide a little of the alpine cuisine.

Look for Specials and Discounts: During certain hours or as part of special campaigns, a lot of restaurants, cable cars, and attractions offer discounts. Look for discounts to make your experience more affordable.

Budget-Friendly Alpine Magic: An All-Age Chamonix Adventure

With its breathtaking mountain scenery, Chamonix entices tourists on a budget while providing a magical experience. Chamonix welcomes you to enjoy the splendor of the Alps without going over budget, whether it's by sampling delicious local food, visiting free sites, or locating comfortable lodging. So get out there, enjoy the tastes of the mountains, and let Charmonix's spirit charm you as you travel affordably through this enchanted mountain retreat.

KEY LOCATIONS AND LANDMARKS:
Navigating Charmonix's Alpine Tapestry

Take a tour of the main attractions and sites in Chamonix, where the Alps display their splendor and the town's charm is shown from every angle. Let's investigate the well-known locations that characterize this captivating destination's alpine charm.

1. The "**Needle of the South**" is the Aiguille du Midi (Place de l'Aiguille du Midi, 45.9035° N, 6.8879° E). It is the ultimate alpine experience. An exciting cable car trip will take you to the peak, where you may stand at 3,842 meters above sea level. The expansive vistas of Mont Blanc and the neighboring summits are breathtaking. Make arrangements for your cable car journey at reservations@compagniedumontblanc.fr for a once-in-a-lifetime experience.

2. **Mont Blanc (Many Viewpoints):** Towering magnificently above Chamonix, Mont Blanc (45.8325° N, 6.8655° E) is the highest peak in the Alps. From vantage points like Le Brévent (45.9326° N, 6.8659° E) or Aiguille du Midi, take in its splendor. Consider cable car trips or

guided excursions (info@lebrevent.com and info@aiguilledumidi.net) to improve your viewing experience.

3. **Le Brévent (45.9326° N, 6.8659° E):** Climb to the summit of Le Brévent for stunning views of the Mont Blanc range and the Chamonix Valley. The ride on the cable car is an experience in and of itself, and the view from the top is breathtaking. You may reserve a cable car by contacting info@lebrevent.com.

4. **Rue du Docteur Paccard (Town Center):** Stroll along this busy main street to get a sense of the bustling core of Chamonix (45.9235° N, 6.8687° E). This street, lined with quaint stores, warm cafés, and boutiques for the mountains, perfectly encapsulates the lively spirit of the town. Take in the alpine beauty and discover hidden gems in the area.

5. **Saint-Michel Église (Église Place, 45.9229° N, 6.8685° E):** Experience the rich history of the town by visiting Église Saint-Michel. This charming church serves as a representation of Charmonix's rich cultural history with its unusual spire. See the inside of the church and go to services to get a sense of the neighborhood. Please email info@eglise-chamonix.fr with any questions.

6. Parc Couttet (45.9221° N, 6.8692° E): With Mont Blanc as a background, this public park offers peace. Nestled among lush mountain foliage, unwind by the immaculate waters. Bring a picnic basket and have an affordable dinner while admiring the expansive views of the famous peaks.

7. Plan de l'Aiguille (45.9202° N, 6.8696° E): This midway point to Aiguille du Midi provides breathtaking views in a tranquil environment. It is accessible by cable car, and it offers hiking opportunities as well as a chance to see the sun rise or set over the mountains.

8. Chamonix Outdoor Market: At the Chamonix outdoor market (Place du Mont Blanc, 45.9231° N, 6.8693° E), indulge your senses. This market (open on certain days) in the town center features alpine specialties, handmade products, and local vegetables. Take in the lively environment without paying an admission cost.

9. Chamonix Alpine Museum: Visit the Chamonix Alpine Museum (89 Avenue Michel Croz, 45.9221° N, 6.8692° E) to learn about the history of alpine exploration. Explore artifacts, images, and stories that chart the history of mountaineering in the area. Please email info@musee-alpin-chamonix.fr for information about museum hours and guided tours.

10. **Maison de la Montagne**: Discover this mountain enthusiast center, located at 100 Immeuble le Chamois, 45.9226° N, 6.8695° E. Attend lectures, seminars, and cultural events to get insight into the alpine way of life. Ask the helpful staff about events happening in the area. Use info@maisondelamontagne.org to get in contact.

Enhancing Your Exploration: Tips for Immersive Adventures

Take into consideration these pointers to improve your exploration and make lasting memories while you visit Charmonix's important places and landmarks:

Guided Excursions: For a deeper understanding of the ecological and cultural importance of famous locations like Aiguille du Midi or Mont Blanc, choose guided excursions.

Taste the local cuisine by visiting the cafés and eateries on Rue du Docteur Paccard. Talk to locals to find hidden jewels that will give you a genuine experience of alpine cuisine.

Seasonal Considerations: In particular during the winter, confirm the accessibility and opening times of the attractions. There may be seasonal differences in certain cable cars and vistas.

Photography Essentials: Equip yourself with the necessary equipment to capture Charmonix's beauty. Make sure your camera is prepared to capture the breathtaking views forever.

Cultural Immersion: To meet people who share your interests in mountains and get fully immersed in the local way of life, check out the activities and seminars held at Maison de la Montagne.

Unveiled at Chamonix: An Alpine Marvel Tapestry
The main sites and attractions of Chamonix invite you to discover the town's rich history, vibrant culture, and breathtaking natural surroundings. Every place adds a colorful thread to the tale of Chamonix, whether you're standing atop the Aiguille du Midi, meandering along Rue du Docteur Paccard, or exploring the alpine tradition at Maison de la Montagne. Now go on this trip across the mountains, take in the majesty of the peaks, and let each landmark serve as a new chapter in your Chamonix experience.

HUT ETIQUETTE: Navigating Alpine Hospitality with Grace

Set off on an adventure through Charmonix's mountain cabins, where warmth and altitude collide. It is essential to comprehend hut etiquette to guarantee a peaceful and delightful stay in these mountain retreats. Come explore the unspoken rules that govern hut life with me, and we'll up the ante on your alpine experience.

1. The first is the Refuge du Plan de l'Aiguille (located at 45.9202° N and 6.8696° E): Hikers and climbers may find a comfortable place to stay at Refuge du Plan de l'Aiguille, which is located at a height of 2,208 meters. You may send an email to info@refugeduplandelaiguille-Bellevue.com to make a reservation and get more information.

2. Refuge du Lac Blanc (Lac Blanc, 45.9291° N, 6.8612° E): This 2,352-meter refuge provides a tranquil haven with views of the immaculate waters of Lac Blanc. Email refuge.lacblanc@wanadoo.fr for bookings and pricing information.

3. At 2,516 meters above sea level, Refuge du Requin (Montenvers, 45.9023° N, 6.8743° E) serves as a base for alpinists visiting the Mer de Glace. Contact info@refugedurequin.com for bookings and pricing information.

The Art of Alpine Hospitality: Hut Etiquette Unveiled

a. Reservations and communication

Reservations Should Be Made Well in Advance: Since space is limited, it is advised to make reservations well in advance, particularly during popular seasons. To reserve your space, get in touch with the hut via phone or email. Unambiguous Communication When making a reservation, be sure to include any specific needs or dietary restrictions. This guarantees that the personnel at the hut can meet your requirements.

b. Take Care of Your Space and Pack Lightly

The minimalist approach is to bring just the necessities since alpine lodges are small. Bring personal stuff, toiletries, and a small sleeping bag. Store extra items in approved storage facilities or at lower elevations.

Respect Common Areas: Exercise caution while using shared spaces. Organize your possessions and refrain from bringing personal objects into your sleeping quarters.

c. **Quiet Hours and Lights Out:**

Respect Sleep Cycles: To guarantee that everyone has a restful night's sleep, lights out and quiet times are essential. Observe the time slots and, in the nighttime, utilize headlamps or very little lights.

d. **Dining Etiquette**

Common Dining: Huts usually include common places for people to eat together. Accept the sense of community and strike up a discussion with other hikers.

After a meal, clear the table and put away any used dishes in their proper places. This aids in the effective cleaning efforts made by the hut workers.

e. Toilet Facilities

Observe the Rules: Alpine lodges sometimes have few restrooms. Use designated places for personal hygiene and abide by water consumption standards.

Be patient and kind to those who may be waiting to use the facilities during periods of high use.

f. Waste Management

Pack Out Waste and Adhere to the Leave No Trace philosophy. Remove any garbage from the area, such as wrappers and non-biodegradable materials. Facilities for recycling could be available; make appropriate use of them.

Mindful Disposal: To reduce your influence on the environment, carefully follow any composting or trash disposal instructions that the hut may provide.

g. Community Spirit

Socialize Responsibly: Have fun interacting with others, but keep others in mind. While some visitors may love being alone, others might prefer companionship. Observe personal preferences.

Assist those Hikers: Provide support to those hikers in need. In the alpine environment, collaboration and exchange of experiences are vital.

h. Environmental Stewardship

Remain on Marked paths: To reduce your influence on the environment, stay on marked paths. Respect the habitats of animals and refrain from trampling on sensitive plants. Learn for Yourself: To appreciate the fragile alpine ecology, educate yourself about the local flora and wildlife. Adhere to the hut staff's recommendations for appropriate alpine conduct.

i. Gratitude and Feedback

Thank the hut staff for their hospitality and express your appreciation. A modest token of appreciation goes a long way toward recognizing their work.

Constructive Feedback: Please share any constructive criticism you may have. Huts often value suggestions to improve the visitor experience.

Enhancing Your Alpine Experience: Hut Etiquette Advice

To guarantee a smooth and enjoyable experience as you immerse yourself in the alpine warmth of Charmonix's huts, take into account these suggestions:

Examine Hut Policies: Become acquainted with the unique regulations, norms, and policies that apply to each hut. This aids in meeting their particular needs.

Prepare Enough: Bring necessary gear, such as a sleeping bag, flashlight, and clothes that fit. Being well-prepared helps ensure a relaxing visit.

Recognize Cultural Differences: Huts could draw customers from throughout the world. Accept cultural variety and have an open mind to new ideas.

Keep Up: Stay informed about trail conditions, weather, and any pertinent information that the hut staff may supply.

This guarantees that the selections you make on your trip are well-informed.

Conscientious Photography: When taking pictures, respect other people's privacy. When taking pictures of other hikers, get their permission and refrain from using flash in sleeping regions.

A Symphony of Alpine Hospitality: Navigating Huts with Finesse

The mountain lodges of Chamonix provide a special fusion of adventure and hospitality. Adopting proper hut etiquette makes you a valuable member of the mountain community and adds to a peaceful and enjoyable trip. Let the spirit of alpine etiquette lead you as you travel across the high-altitude terrain and relax in the comfortable confines of these refuges, making every hut a memorable chapter in your story of Charmonix's towering peaks.

NAVIGATION: A Guide Through Charmonix's Alpine Wonderland

Charmonix's scenic landscapes demand a combination of practical knowledge and an adventurous attitude to navigate. Whether you're walking along Rue du Docteur Paccard or reaching the heights of Aiguille du Midi, let's make sure your trip through this Alps is smooth and delightful.

Practical Navigation Tips

Signage & path Markers: Chamonix has a vast hiking path system. Pay close attention to trail markings and signs. Important landmarks such as Plan de l'Aiguille (45.9202° N, 6.8696° E) serve as landmarks.

Offline Maps: To keep oriented, particularly in distant places, utilize GPS devices or download offline maps. Useful apps for offline navigation include Maps.me and other similar ones.

Weather Considerations: Pay close attention to weather predictions, particularly before heading out on mountain paths. Weather patterns may be unpredictable, which might affect trail safety and visibility.

Local Guides: If you're traveling for the first time or have difficult routes, think about hiring a local guide. They improve your whole experience and provide insights into the landscape.

Contacts for Emergencies: Keep emergency numbers on your phone, such as the number for the local mountain rescue services (PGHM Chamonix: +33 4 50 53 16 89). Always be ready for the unexpected.

Useful Contacts

The tourist information center is located at 85 Place du Triangle de l'Amitié, 45.9236° N, 6.8698° E. It is the main hub for maps, help, and information. Send questions to info@chamonix.com via email.

Cable cars and lifts may help you enhance your journey in Chamonix Mont-Blanc. For bookings, send an email to info@compagniedumontblanc.fr to Compagnie du Mont-Blanc.

Hospital Chamonix (77 Avenue du Mont-Blanc, 45.9293°
N, 6.8706° E): You may contact the Chamonix Hospital at
+33 4 50 53 10 33 in the event of an emergency.

Chamonix Police Station (8 Route de la Pia, 45.9347° N,
6.8672° E): Call +33 4 50 53 77 77 for non-emergency help
from the local police.

35 Place de la Mer de Glace, 45.9238° N, 6.8740° E) is the
Petit Train du Montenvers. Take a ride on the quaint
mountain train. Contact contact@montenvers.fr for
bookings and timetables.

Glossary Local Terms

The French word "**needle**," Aiguille, is often employed in
mountain names such as Aiguille du Midi.

Refuge: A mountain cabin or climbing/hiking shelter.
Refuge du Lac Blanc and Refuge du Plan de l'Aiguille are
two examples.

Mont is the French word meaning "mount." One
well-known example is the summit of the Alps, Mont Blanc.

PGHM: Haute Montagne Gendarmerie Peloton. In Chamonix, the High Mountain Gendarmerie Squadron offers mountain rescue services.

Alpage: A high-altitude grassland that is often used in the summer to graze animals.

Col: A saddle or mountain pass that separates two summits.

Télécabine, which translates to "cable car" in French, is a typical way to go to high-altitude locations.

Buvette: A little alpine refreshment station or café that's ideal for a stroll.

Improving Your Alpine Adventure: How to Get Around Chamonix

Take into account these pointers as you set out on your mountain journey to improve your understanding of Charmonix's navigation:

Keep Up to Date: Continually monitor trail conditions, weather reports, and closure announcements. Local tourist information offices are excellent sources of information.

Equipment Check: Make sure all of your navigational tools, including GPS units and maps, are operational. Before you go, familiarize yourself with their usage.

Cultural Courtesy: Be mindful of regional traditions, particularly in rural places. Observe proper trail protocol and engage in polite conversation with locals.

Follow the Leave No Trace guidelines to reduce your environmental effects. Keep paths clean and show respect for animal habitats.

Make Connections with Locals: Talk to locals to learn about their hidden treasures and subtle cultural differences. They often provide insightful advice and suggestions.

Chamonix Navigation: A Harmony of Hills & Valleys
Discover the charm of the French Alps by traveling through Charmonix's varied landscapes, which entice travelers to explore its peaks and valleys. You're prepared to explore this alpine splendor with helpful contacts, a dictionary of local words, and helpful navigation suggestions. May the beauty of Chamonix be revealed to you at every turn, and may the delight of discovery accompany you on your trip through this enthralling mountain retreat.

CONCLUSION: Embracing Charmonix's Alpine Splendors

As our mountain adventure through Chamonix comes to an end, you have experienced the imposing peaks, charming town squares, and hospitable cottages that characterize this enchanted location. Every area contributes a different color to the tapestry of Chamonix, from the tranquil waters of Lac Blanc to the expansive views of the Aiguille du Midi.

Remember, for future adventures

Make Easy Reservations: Arrange your visit by booking accommodations in well-known shelters such as Refuge du Plan de l'Aiguille (info@refugeduplandelaiguille-Bellevue.com).

For a restful night's sleep at 2,352 meters, embrace simplicity in shelters like Refuge du Lac Blanc (refuge.lacblanc@wanadoo.fr). Pack light, and sleep well.

Etiquette Matters: At Refuge du Requin (info@refugedurequin.com), navigate hut life with elegance and adherence to the unwritten laws.

By keeping in mind latitudes, longitudes, and polite behavior, you'll be ready for a memorable mountain trip in Chamonix. May the memories of the expansive vistas and the welcoming hut hospitality remain as you say adieu to this mountain retreat, beckoning you back to Charmonix's alpine embrace. I hope your next trips are infused with the spirit of the French Alps and that you have safe travels.

FREQUENTLY ASKED QUESTIONS

Starting an alpine trek in Chamonix piques interest. In this section, we answer often-asked concerns to make sure your trip is clear and exciting.

Q1. When is the ideal time to visit Chamonix?

A1: While winter (December to March) draws skiers, summer (June to September) is the best period for trekking and exploration. Before your journey, check the trail conditions and weather predictions.

Q2: How can I book a trip to Aiguille du Midi via cable car?

A2: Send an email to info@compagniedumontblanc.fr to reserve your place with Compagnie du Mont-Blanc. Make sure to reserve well in advance, particularly during popular times.

Q3: How much does a stay at Refuge du Lac Blanc cost?

A3: Contact refuge.lacblanc@wanadoo.fr for reservations and costs for lodging. They'll provide information on prices and facilities that are offered.

Q4: Can I hike without a guide to Lac Blanc?

A4: Yes, individual hikers may reach Lac Blanc. Observe designated paths and contemplate the use of GPS units or offline maps. Before you go, check the weather and trail conditions.

Q5: How can I get in touch with PGHM Chamonix in an emergency?

A5: Call PGHM Chamonix at +33 4 50 53 16 89 in case of emergency. to get in touch with them for mountain rescue services, save this number on your phone.

Q6: Are there any budget-friendly dining options in Chamonix?

A6: Absolutely, check out the quaint cafés and reasonably priced restaurants on Rue du Docteur Paccard. Talk to locals to find affordable hidden treasures.

Q7: What are Charmonix's outdoor activity safety regulations?

A7: Learn about safety precautions, particularly for rafting, paragliding, and mountain riding. For knowledgeable guidance on each activity, get in touch with local guides.

Q8: Is it possible to sum up Chamonix in a budget?

A8: Definitely! Visit Parc Couttet (45.9221° N, 6.8692° E) for an affordable day in the heart of the alpine scenery. For an unforgettable trip, enjoy reasonably priced local food and explore free sights.

Q9: How can I get a seat at an event hosted by Maison de la Montagne?

A9: Send an email to info@maisondelamontagne.org about events and seminars at Maison de la Montagne. They will provide you with information about forthcoming events and how to secure a seat.

Q10: For greater comprehension, where can I get a dictionary of regional terms?

A10: For information about the Tourist Information Center at Chamonix (45.9236° N, 6.8698° E), see the Useful Contacts section. They may provide you with information on local words or point you in the direction of local resources.

Your Chamonix Adventure Unveiled: More Questions?
Please email info@chamonix.com to the Tourist Information Center if you have any further queries or would need individualized suggestions for your trip to Chamonix. Their friendly crew is prepared to help you easily navigate the Alps. Your inquisitiveness drives the thrill of discovery in Chamonix - may your voyage be full of amazement and learning among the magnificent French Alps!

Printed in Great Britain
by Amazon